AMSTERDAM

This book was devised and produced by
Multimedia Publications (UK) Ltd

Editor: Marilyn Inglis
Production: Arnon Orbach
Design: John Strange and Associates
Picture Research: Sheila Corr

First published in the United States of
America 1985 by Gallery Books, an imprint of
W. H. Smith Publishers Inc., 112 Madison
Avenue, New York, NY 10016.

ISBN 0 8317 0316 4

Origination by Imago
Printed in Italy by Sagdos, Milan
Typeset by Flowery Typesetters Ltd.

AMSTERDAM

Michael Leech

GALLERY BOOKS

An Imprint of W. H. Smith Publishers Inc.

112 Madison Avenue

New York City 10016

Contents

Amsterdam – City on the Water

Amsterdam is one of those cities travelers always go back to. It has a quality that evokes nostalgic memories, and an impact few can resist. It has often been called, in that banal, travel-brochure way, "the Venice of the North", sometimes sharing the description with its smaller Belgian neighbor, Bruges, which is also built along canals. Amsterdam is no more like Venice than Venice is like Amsterdam, however: the city is uniquely itself. It may be built upon water and marsh, as is Venice, but there the similarity ends. Amsterdam is the product of Dutch abilities and Dutch imagination. It may have its feet in the water, but its head is firmly in the air.

For the visitor who has been there before the city extends the same well-remembered welcome; to those lucky enough to be seeing it for the first time it is full of delicious surprises, the kind of pleasures that travel used to bring in so many now-spoiled spots. Time and the twentieth century have changed Amsterdam, but it still remains resolutely itself, unlike its Dutch sister city, Rotterdam, which was almost completely destroyed in World War II, and has risen phoenix-like as an advanced, totally modern city. Spared the havoc of war for the most part, Amsterdam retains the gilded trappings of a seventeenth- and eighteenth-century city at its heart, yet it is as lively and as innovative as today in its population and in its attitudes.

So what will the present-day visitor find in this unusual city with its waterborne life? A great deal to do and see, and a vital and lively flow of people wherever he or she looks. The people who live there are very proud of their home, and invariably will reveal a considerable knowledge of its culture, background and history. It is useful and interesting for the first-time visitor to have some knowledge of these subjects, for they will give a foundation on which to build knowledge and awareness. And in talking with the people – a vital part of the process of getting to know any town – you

Water, water everywhere – in Amsterdam you are always close to a canal. These old houses with their typical stepped gables are caught reflected in the still water.

will give pleasure and surprise when you reveal your newly acquired knowledge of this city on the water.

Amsterdam began as a small fishing settlement about a thousand years ago when a few settlers built wooden shacks at the meeting of the Amstel and the lj rivers. To protect the little hamlet from the ever-menacing sea they dammed the Amstel to create a sea wall – hence the name, of course. Somewhere under the majestic expanse of the central Dam Square must be the original blockage of the river, for the city fanned out in all directions from these simple beginnings. Located as it was, the village had importance as a strategically sited trade center, and it was not long before markets sprang up and businesses other than fishing began. Soon little Amsterdam became a free port with special toll concessions, making it even more attractive, and it began to grow quickly. The new city thrived in its waterborne position, and four centuries ago a major program of development began with the construction of the central canals. There was first a little one, little more than a moat, near the Dam along the Voorburgwal, but later development added crescents of canals, one inside the other, so that shipping could sail right into the city and cargoes could be taken off in the center, making for easy transfer and a safer transit. If you look at the map of Amsterdam you will see that the main center is a series of U-shaped roads and canals with the open end towards the water. Although there is now a great spread of suburbs beyond the central city, this old part is still the vital heart, a crowded, jostling mass where it seems everyone wants to be!

Above Although the city has changed vastly, many old buildings survive – the Straddling Tower (Schreierstower) can be seen at the edge of the settlement in the map opposite. Here it can be seen in its modern setting with the baroque outline of the church of St Nicholas behind.

Right The ancient heart of Amsterdam, where it all began a thousand years ago, is now the Dam Square – and still the center of the city. It makes a splendid open space for crowds to congregate, especially on warm weekends.

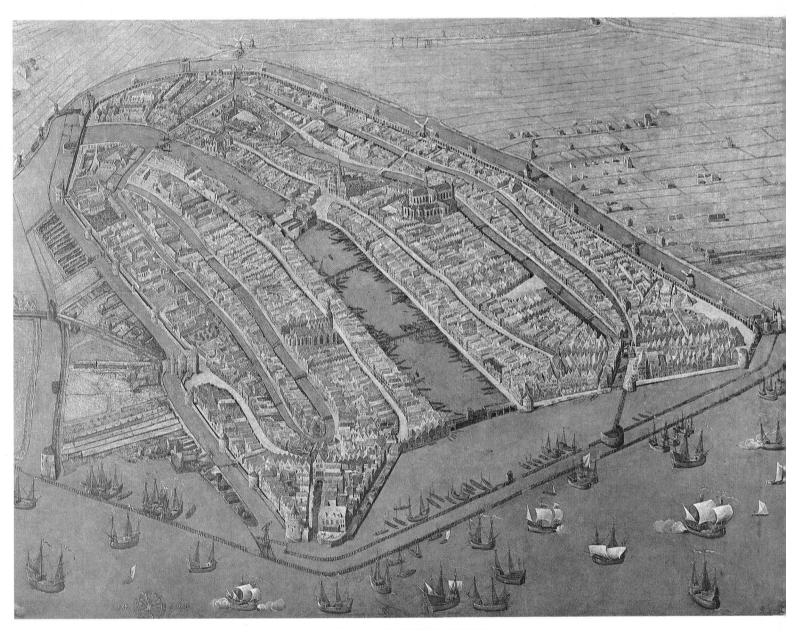

Above This map of Amsterdam shows how the heart of the city was shaped more than three centuries ago. Already a plan of looped canals has emerged, and the new city's importance as a port is underlined with the many ships, lighters and barges.

Left Fishing is still a business in Holland, but usually practiced far away in the North Sea with modern ships. Here a solitary fisherman casts his net from his own small outboard motor boat.

9

In the seventeenth century the Dutch finally shook off the Spanish yoke. They had been forced to accept unpalatable indignities, notably many attempts to crush a deeply cherished Protestantism. This was the Spaniards' undoing. In 1609 a truce was signed and eventually in 1648 the Spanish withdrew and the provinces of the Netherlands were at last independent. There had been many struggles, battles and more than a few deaths, but with a surge of confidence the new country embarked on what is now known as "the Golden Age". Amsterdam was the central originator of a new vitality which swept the population into an era of exploration and robust trade with far-off countries in both the East and West.

Amsterdam was not a society of aristocrats, as were so many other European cities. It had a strong, hard-headed merchant class living in large if narrow houses on the canals, often with the warehouse on the top floor and the family living below. These houses are one of the glories of present-day Amsterdam — hundreds of them still line the canals, and their grand large-windowed façades are reflected in the still, green water of the canals. At first this vital new city had a ruler and a royal line, culminating in a King William who became William III of England. When he died without heirs Holland became a republic, and over the next century the country alternated between being a monarchy and a republic, eventually gaining its present shape after 1830 with the formation of the modern Belgium. Holland was neutral during the American Revolution and during World War I. In World War II the country was invaded and occupied by the Nazis, during which time, despite much strenuous protest, many citizens of Holland were deported, including a large number of Jews, and sent for slave labor and eventual death in the concentration camps. Although the Netherlands is a modern, forward-thinking country, it doesn't forget its past, and Amsterdam has many reminders of the terrible war years of 1939 to 1945.

Right Even newer houses in Amsterdam have an age-old problem — how to get the furniture in, for stairways are often narrow and precipitous, to take up as little precious space as possible. A hook and tackle is often used, and the extra-large windows help access for bigger articles.

Right You won't often see wooden clogs being worn in Holland today, except in some rural villages and for special occasions. Here someone has made them into a decoration beside two typically lace-curtained windows.

Below The Dutch like a comfy sense of clutter – or else they go for a bare, modern look. Old houses often have the cozy, curtained look of this one.

Right Under an old hoist the crumbling brown brick is being attended to by a house-holder. Above is a glimpse of one of the city's beautiful scrolled and curved plaster gable ends, each one different and some splendidly detailed.

Although Amsterdam is the capital, the government sits in The Hague, and the latter town is also where the present Queen Beatrix and her family live. The large Royal Palace on the Dam Square is no longer a residence. Amsterdam is still a vital commercial city, and Holland is very much a part of modern Europe – it is a leading member of the European Economic Community or Common Market and has grown – its current population now stands at 14 million and new suburbs have spread over the flat lands. Amsterdam has added new amenities, including a subway, and the airport of Schiphol serves the city with a large number of international flights every day, as well as being the home of KLM, Royal Dutch Airlines. Amsterdam is a major tourist attraction for other European countries, and this is a year-round business so the city is never quiet. Yet you can still find silent, calm places within this city where water laps against mossy quaysides, and frequent sea mists remind you that the ocean, Amsterdam's oldest ally-and-enemy, is never very far away.

Facing page In every available corner the bicycles of Amsterdam are parked – pedal power is important in this city of restricted access. Behind can be seen a typical narrow canal house, and posters of current goings-on around the town.

Below Rush hour in Amsterdam means the whizz of cycle wheels. There are special routes mapped out for cycles all over Holland, indicated by blue-and-white circular markers.

Bottom With so many cycles, repair shops are found all over the city, and bicycles must get a bumping with so many cobbled streets to negotiate. You can rent machines at very reasonable rates from such places, and also from rail stations.

Gleamingly lit with thousands of light bulbs, the bridges of Amsterdam provide a fairy-tale spectacle at night. This elaborate drawbridge, all illuminated, crosses the Amstel River on the edge of the old city.

Right Without a doubt this is the favorite statue of Amsterdam people – this boy of the backstreets has been well captured by the sculptor, and his stance and expression have given him the title of 'the cheeky lad'.

Below The innovative ideas of Holland's museums will be appreciated – here lockers from a former orphanage are used as a background display in the Historical Museum.

Facing page Set as if in motion, these suits of 300-year-old armor seem much more interesting than the usual correct, stiff presentations. They are also easy to see, flooded with daylight in one of the Historical Museum's wide galleries.

The City – Origins and Present-day

In the first chapter we saw that Amsterdam is a town built on a series of canals – well, everyone knows that! It's probably the image everyone summons up when they think about Amsterdam. The interesting thing is, however, that although these waterways now reflect stately town houses and lazily floating swans, they were *not* built for their charm and picturesque effect. Nowadays they are splendid for tourists, but they started life as busy commercial channels, crowded with boats, barges, lighters, skiffs and even many-sailed ships.

The hard-headed businessman of Amsterdam wanted to conduct his business as close to the goods as he could, and since Amsterdam is at sea level – parts are even below it – it was not difficult for craft to ride right into the city if channels were provided. In time the canals were built, the first as a kind of straight moat in the middle of the city, making a lozenge-shaped piece of land with one end at what is now the railway station (with, beyond, the water of the Ijsselmeer stretching away to the North Sea) and the other at the Muntplein. Here are the most ancient parts of the city, and the names reflect the age of the place – the Voorburgwal means "Before the City Moat" and two parallel thoroughfares with canals down the middle are called Oude Zijds Voorburgwal, or "Old Moat Side", and Nieuwe Zijds Voorburgwal, "New Moat Side". This is a fascinating part of Amsterdam – you see the life of the city before you, from the local people shopping to the busy sex bar on the opposite bank! Amsterdam is indeed a city of contrasts.

Beyond these two central canals are looped the others. The Singel is the first one you come to as you walk from the Dam Square heading west. Then, like a series of crescents each larger than the other, come the three principal canals. These are the canals that invite the strollers – they are in order (after the Singel), The Herengracht (or Gentlemen's Canal); the Keizersgracht (Kings' Canal); the Prinsengracht (Princes' Canal). A fourth, the Singelgracht,

Previous page A pleasure boat negotiates a curve in a canal. You can take a short cruise around Amsterdam in one of these wide-windowed craft and see the city from water level – an ideal introduction to Holland's principal city.

Top right This modern aerial photograph gives a very good gull's-eye impression of the city today. With open water beyond, the old city is contained within the five concentric half circles of the original seventeenth century canals. The city continues to spread fan-wise into its newer outer suburbs, practically all at sea-level.

Center right On the quieter canals beyond the busy center you will find birds on the quaysides and on the water, while old trees leaning over the canal make attractive prospects for the painter, or for the camera enthusiast.

effectively belts in the old city and marks its division from the suburbs.

Along these lovely waterways the Amsterdam entrepreneur of the seventeenth century conducted business. You can see what the burgers looked like from their portraits in the Rijksmuseum – dour, plain and simply dressed, their faces stare out of numerous canvases to proclaim their strength of purpose and their piety. Since houses were taxed on their width and land was very valuable, they built narrow, tall houses; and hoists were set in the gables to lift cargoes from the boats below. Amsterdam is all marsh, so buildings could not be vast and the long terraces of town houses are all clumped together, holding each other up. The buildings often have magnificent façades, and sometimes the most extraordinary gables, stepped, scrolled and gilded, so that you could spend an entire holiday in the city just strolling around and looking at the upper floors. Every gable is different and they add a touch of the fantastic to the cobbled quaysides and cinnamon-colored brick fronts of the houses. The houses are indeed the essence of Amsterdam, and you can even stay in one, for many have been converted into hotels. Rigid laws forbid the despoiling of this grand architectural heritage, so "façadism" as practiced in other countries (whereby a building's front is preserved while its interior is rebuilt) has not ruined many buildings here. One hotel has actually been converted from 19 old houses into a mazy up-and-down and thoroughly delightful hotel – individual rooms still retain their original look and atmosphere.

Facing page, bottom Forced out of housing which is expensive in central Amsterdam, many city-dwellers have taken to the water. There are houseboats of all sizes and ages along many of the canals. Surprisingly spacious, some even have roof gardens!

Left "More window than wall' was an epithet applied to a Tudor palace in England – but it applies even more to the houses of old Amsterdam, where bricks often seem a mere edging to acres of glass. This is a typical street corner across a bridge.

Above Although the houses of Amsterdam are generally practical and plain they often bear endearing and colorful sculptures and panels, as though even the burghers of a city built on business had to find places to express a little exuberance – seen most of all of course in such curly eave decorations as this.

Left The Herengracht is the grandest canal, with an array of town-houses of the merchants on both sides of its waterway. Confined by space restrictions, the houses are narrow but make up for their limited façades with sculpted doorways and grandly carved and polished doors, like this one.

Right Not all doorways are palatial – this neat black door with its brightly polished brass knocker probably leads on to a narrow staircase – for as you can see the neighboring door is jammed against the steep stone steps. It is to be found on the Singel canal.

Good strong shoes are a necessity in Amsterdam, or else a bicycle – for to see these architectural glories you will need to walk along the quays and over the little hump-backed bridges. Old Amsterdam is also a city of open spaces, for while the Dutch were careful with their reclaimed land (they have added to the size of their country by more than a fifth of the present total area since the early nineteenth century by dragging back land from the North Sea), they also appreciated having room to look around. Amsterdam has a number of squares or "pleins" at strategic points for the exercise and pleasure of its citizens. Besides the central Dam Square with its imposing Royal Palace and the Nieuwe Kerk you have the Waterlooplein, the Rembrandtsplein with the neighboring Thorbeckeplein, busy with strollers and full of cafés, the Muntplein, the Nieuwe Markt and the Leidseplein, close to the theaters, and of course the big and rather bare square in front of the ugly Central Station, the Stationplein. There are no parks in central Amsterdam – the residents have some gardens, it's true, but they are often tiny, and so there are windowboxes all over the place, showing the Dutch pleasure in growing things. Parks are found outside the old city, and they are very agreeable – the Vondelpark for example, just beyond the outer ring of the Singelgracht, is large and has lots of grass and trees.

The soft ground did not stop the Dutch from building vast churches, and these add exclamation points all over the city's skyline, which is in general blessedly unbroken with tall new constructions. You can also see some of the city's fortifications where the canals front the sea. It is certainly interesting to travel beyond the old center and into the suburbs, and the buses are easy to ride. The ticket gives a certain journey time, so keep it for the duration of your trip for transfers. If you decide to rent a bicycle you will find that the Dutch are beautifully organized when it comes to this mode of transport, and there

Bottom There are several important buildings on the Dam Square. Here is the so-called Royal Palace, which is *not* inhabited by the royal family. Beside it is the handsome Nieuwe Kerk, or 'new church' to differentiate it from the 'old' one. Its interior and its handsome carvings are well worth exploring.

Below Inside the Royal Palace are suites of apartments – it was once the palace of a king, Napoleon's brother, but was for long the Town Hall. Here is the Burgersaal, or Citizens' Hall, imposing and grand. You can visit the palace on most days for a small entrance fee.

are cycle tracks everywhere, marked with a special blue sign with a bicycle on it.

The fathers of Amsterdam created a working city which in the twentieth century has become something of an anachronism, for these fine buildings are of course no longer used for their original purposes. In recent decades, however, it has become very fashionable to live in an old canal house and the properties have become extremely expensive. There are many problems involved in keeping the houses and the canals in good order, and a tightly packed population does not help matters. The attitude of the Amsterdam City Council is to do all that it can to preserve the fabric of the city, for this is a reflection in brick, stone and wood of what Amsterdamers created as their place to live, and today's citizens are eager to keep the city as much as possible the same.

Right Summer in the city, and the fine tower and crowned spire of the Westerkerk is seen along a shady canal. Holland's church spires are unique, and often very tall as if to rise as much as possible over the flat countryside.

Below No doubt the old lady feels she is doing a kindly act in feeding the pigeons, but in Amsterdam, as in many other cities, there are so many of them damaging the stonework of old buildings that they are really urban pests.

Left Most of the canals of Amsterdam are divided from the houses by narrow quaysides and paved streets. Here, behind the Damrak, the water laps right up against the house fronts.

Below Inside the Nieuwe Kerk are splendid windows. Try to choose a bright day to visit the interior so that you can appreciate the vibrant color and intricate design of such medieval stained glass as this.

Below A view that little Anne Frank may have seen from her attic – a typical backstreet look at tall gables and red-tiled roofs.

Near right Here you get a real impression of the way Amsterdam is crowded in on itself – Holland is a tightly populated country, and in Amsterdam people live and work in the closest proximity to each other.

Far right Flowers are very important in Amsterdam. You can see barges loaded with them by the Singel, and besides cut flowers there are pot-plants and bedding-plants available too, as you can see from this craft's colorful cargo.

Right When the skies are clear (and it has to be pointed out that it rains just as much in Holland as it does in any country of Northern Europe!) the white painted window frames and gables stand out crisply against the blue.

Right With such a huddlement of houses ordinary tasks can be a problem – as can be seen from the washing suspended from these windows. Pollution, from objects carelessly dropped into the slow-moving canals, also poses major difficulties.

Facing page, top Sculpture and the arts are important to the people of Amsterdam. You'll see many examples of the culture of Holland all over the city, old and modern. Here statues in seventeenth-century dress look over the harbor.

Facing page, bottom Spare walls don't often stay bare long in Amsterdam. Someone with an eye for the visual possibility will soon come along with brushes and ladders to convert bricks to paintings, sometimes realistic and sometimes naïf like this example.

Below Brilliant detail picks up the light in Amsterdam, where due to the presence of so much water you will find a particularly soft illumination, whether on house-fronts or on signs such as this blazing sun, an insurance mark.

Above Small, brightly colored plaques mark parts of ancient Amsterdam with vivid little scenes in low relief like this. The Oude Schans is a section of the central part of Amsterdam.

3
Walking in Old Amsterdam

Compact and neat, Amsterdam is easy for walking – the streets and all directions are well marked, and it's all flat! The only climbing you will need to do is over some of the older bridges. Assuming you are staying somewhere in central Amsterdam (there are hotels big and small throughout the old center) you can strike out in almost any direction and find fascinating things. Here are a few that you shouldn't miss, plus others that will delight and intrigue you, for Amsterdam is a city of surprises. A big surprise is the ever-helpful and useful VVV – the Netherlands Tourist Information Bureau.

They go all out to help the tourist in Amsterdam, and a visit to the office in front of the Central Station is a very sensible move. Maps, brochures and timetables are all there, plus helpful assistants who all speak fluent English. They will even plan or suggest walks for you, and after a visit here the chances are that you will have more things to do than time allows!

Start at the oldest part – the inner Voorburgwal with its quiet waterways – and those famous pink-lit windows where Amsterdam's prostitutes are settled. In most places they would be called "ladies of

the night", but here it seems the world's oldest profession goes on all the time – one of them told me that they work eight-hour shifts round the clock! Many Dutch people come here to gape at the bizarrely-costumed women, and the whole area has become a tourist attraction. Unlike similar parts of other European cities, the area is not dangerous, although drugs are a problem.

The city has become the capital of the European drug trade. Hard drugs are a menace, and to try to control them the Dutch authorities seem to have virtually given up on soft drugs, such as marijuana, which can be procured almost anywhere. Of 3000 police, only 22 work full-time on the drugs beat, so it's hardly surprising that the trade appears to be flourishing.

The Voorburgwal is not all vice, however – look into the handsome old Oude Kerk with it vast brick walls; the historical museum at Kalverstraat; and, perhaps most fascinating of all, the Amstelkring Museum (Oudezijds Voorburgwal 40), where you can see how non-Protestants worshipped when the Reformation refused the opportunity of choice of religion for a

Below Low in the water, prone to all sorts of problems from flooding to rats, yet still a popular home for a city-dweller who will consider himself lucky to have found a home. This old boat shows its age. Inside, however, it is probably very comfortably equipped and is connected to most city services.

time. In general however the Dutch have observed the right of freedom to worship. Here on the upper floor of this merchant's house of 300 years ago is a miniature church, concealed from view, and known to Amsterdamers as "Our Lord in the Attic" – a fascinating place, open every day.

Walk on a bit and you come to Dam Square and the imposing front of the Royal Palace. Stand with your back to the grand hotel which occupies one side of the square and take in the view – there are bound to be many strollers, coming up from the shops in the pedestrianized Kalverstraat, or down from the large mass of the Central Station at the head of the Damrak. Go into the Nieuwe Kerk and admire the carved wood, the chandeliers, and the vast soaring windows. The narrow streets between here and the Station have many small shops and bars, while the big store facing one part of the Dam Square is De Bijenkorf – an attractive and well laid out shop, Amsterdam's biggest department store. The name actually means "the Beehive".

The Central Station area is rather bleak and bare, but here's a tip – you can rent bicycles here by the hour and if you don't want to walk then this is probably the second best way to see the city. Holland's transport system is excellent, and its train service is swift, inexpensive and clean. Trains are frequent and take you to the center of cities, so that you can see them with little delay after a comfortable, quick journey.

Facing page, bottom There are open-air markets all over Amsterdam. Here, in the flea market along Waterlooplein, dozens of bargain-priced articles are laid out for sale.

Below Although there are many antique dealers you will have to look hard to find a bargain in Amsterdam, for the dealers are well aware of the value of good pieces. Here a window in the antique section of the city is cluttered with porcelain.

Right Since the shops have little floorspace goods often spill out onto sidewalks – but it's doubtful that many stores can make such a display as this flower-shop!

Facing page, top The Dutch like to eat well, and although the food is not of grande cuisine level it is hearty and nourishing. All over town, stores offer the gleaming treasure of the many farms that grow fruits and vegetables in the rich flat fields close to Amsterdam's suburbs.

Behind the Royal Palace is the Singel canal, two blocks along the Raadhuisstraat, and you can walk along it; more fascinating though is the Herengracht, the next canal in order. You will want to see the splendid houses that line it along most of the U-shaped loop. They are a parade of beautiful buildings, and what strikes you at once is that although each one is different there is a marvelous sense of uniformity – for all the houses are the same height. This was doubtless imposed by the soft land that they are built upon, but now it gives a lovely series of ordered lines to the ranks of houses. At the tops, these palatial buildings are suddenly given over to the wonderful touches of excess – their plastered gables are florid, fantastical and sometimes quite theatrical! The gables of Amsterdam are one of its greatest pleasures, and you can spend days just gazing up at these varied and imaginative ways of hiding a steep roof.

On the other side of the city, near the busy Waterlooplein, you'll find the house of Rembrandt at 4 Jodenbreestraat, open every day and a restoration of how it looked when the painter actually lived in this seventeenth-century house. At the end of this street you'll find the Botanical Gardens and the Zoo, with the Tropical Museum at the end beyond the Singelgracht. Walk to the Rembrandtsplein and the neighboring Thorbeckeplein for cafés and a busy sense of life at this center of entertainments, from street singers to movie houses. The Munt Tower is nearby and beyond you will find the Singel canal with its flowerboats overflowing onto the cobbled quays, making lovely subjects for photographs. A little way along the Kalverstraat you'll find the turning on the left for Spui – and here is one of the city's surprises – a tiny little concealed green where the almshouses make the square seem like a village. On the next canal, near here, is the Theater Museum. The props, miniature sets, costume sketches and old scenery are framed by the frescoed walls and marble floors of one of the grand houses of this stately canal.

Top Although winter in Amsterdam is frequently wet and overcast, there are fine bright days when you can appreciate the beauty of light reflected from the still waters onto the long lines of house façades, unencumbered by summer leaves.

Bottom There are no locks on the Amsterdam canals for you are at sea level in this waterborne city. There are many bridges, however, and some picturesque ones such as this old lifting bridge.

Above Sometimes the houses are so huddled that they almost seem to be propping each other up! They present a picture of red bricks, red tiles, and white-framed windows. Sometimes house fronts lean out, built that way so that furniture will not bump on the brickwork while being hoisted up.

Left Sometimes there seem to be more bridges than canals! If you think of Amsterdam as being constructed like a spider's web then the streets are the radiating ribs crossing the encircling waterways. And cyclists are to be seen wherever you look, of course.

35

Right A proud householder with only a balcony to use for a garden busily tends his geranuims and petunias. Flower displays such as this make even the darkest streets alive with color.

Below The interior of a typical brown bar, or café. Found all over the city, these agreeable places serve as meeting places and social centers, where you may drink all sorts of beverages, but most popular is beer and the local Genever gin.

Facing page, top The citizen of Holland has always been aware that he has very little space to move in, and being also fond of growing things, even narrow windowledges are pressed into the service of horticulture.

Facing page, bottom Some of the floating residences of Amsterdam are really miniature houses that just happen to be on the water – they certainly never move! Barbecues, lounge chairs and even tomato plants compete for space on built-up 'terraces'.

Along the Prinsengracht is Anne Frank's house at number 263, open every day and still tinged with memories of the sad child whose diaries made so alive the years when Amsterdam, and all Holland, suffered under the Nazi regime. Near here is the huge Westerkerk. Severe and reminiscent of Dutch paintings of the Golden Age inside, its exterior is an Amsterdam landmark. It is open on Tuesday and Thursday afternoons.

Many people want to visit diamond cutting factories in Amsterdam – they are centrally located with the biggest, Van Moppes and Zoon at 2 Albert Cuypstraat, offering a tour and stones on exhibit. Along this street there is an open market every day except Sunday, while for a real flea market try the Waterlooplein every day except Saturday. Look out for another Amsterdam institution while walking – the giant street organs, giving out their unmistakable music and providing another backdrop for photographs. There is usually one near the Leidseplein with its theaters and cafés, opposite the looming Heineken brewery, and close to another great Amsterdam landmark – the florid nineteenth-century palace that houses a fantastic collection of works of art – the Rijksmuseum.

Far left Clogs that once would have clattered along canalsides can now be bought as souvenirs, sometimes to be used as these are as containers for flowers.

Left This nineteenth-century house looks rather like some of the gingerbread hotels that once flourished in the coastal resorts of the USA.

Right The large windows and the brickwork of this frontage are typically Dutch. Brightly painted louvers, or shutters, are seen on many old buildings, and are often practical.

Below The Dutch use their canals for a myriad of purposes apart from the original one of transport. Here is a neatly-encapsulated water-borne chicken farm.

Right The canals need much attention and repair. Here a quayside is being replaced, and most construction is now cement where once wooden piles were used. The canals also silt up with mud and junk, so you will often see dredgers at work.

Below A program to replace quayside roads has been going on for some time, rebuilding worn surfaces and sometimes, as here, using decorative bricks set in sand. It is only because this street is being repaired that there is no rank of tightly-packed cars parked along the canal-side.

Left On some waterways you will see pleasure boats tied up, and even a few working craft to remind you that these canals were once filled with commercial shipping.

4

Art and Religion

The Rijksmuseum is a grandiose palace beyond the wide Stadhouderskade on the edge of the old city. It houses some of the greatest art in the world, with naturally a very strong and complete representation of the Dutch schools, mainly of the seventeenth century. It's essential not to rush a visit here – allow at least half a day, and maybe a return visit, for although there are many famous paintings you will recognize, there are also many rooms that are full of works that will be new to many visitors – some may well become your favorites. There is an entry fee (as there is at most Dutch museums, and some churches), and the gallery is open every day from 10 am to 5 pm and on Sundays from 1 pm to 5 pm. (Most museums are open at these or very similar times.)

Once inside you can wander at will, but there are galleries you should not miss. Dutch art reflects the city even today, so get a guide to the galleries and look on these portraits and pictures of street and home life not just as paintings but as vivid representations of aspects of Dutch life, some of which can still be glimpsed today, particularly on the sidewalks and squares of the smaller cities. The studies of people working, for example, and the faces that Rembrandt and Vermeer painted can still be seen, if you look and let your imagination play its part as you walk through the town.

Both Rembrandt and Vermeer are well represented here – the famous "Night Watch" is situated in solitary grandeur in its own gallery, and there are several famous canvases of Vermeer, of whom very little is known apart from the fact that he lived and worked in Delft. The galleries are neatly laid out, and the paintings are well lit and displayed. But don't limit your visit to the

Right The Dutch enjoy the heritage of art their city encouraged three hundred years ago – but they also appreciate new work. At the Stedelijk a crowd looks at modern Dutch works. The museum also shows modern art from other countries.

paintings – the Rijksmuseum has many other things to see, from massive silver pieces to exquisite lace panels and superb examples of furniture. There is also a very good, plain restaurant and coffee bar where you can rest weary feet between gallery strolls. On Sundays the museums do tend to get crowded – Amsterdamers are proud of their heritage and crush into the galleries on their afternoons off. It is probably best to go at opening time during the week if you want to avoid the crowd.

For those who love modern art, a visit to the Stedelijk Museum (Municipal Museum) on Paulus Potterstraat is a must. Besides examples of new Dutch work there is a very good selection of Impressionist paintings. It's open at the same hours as the Rijksmuseum. There is a museum devoted solely to Van Gogh. It's next door on the Paulus Potterstraat and can't be missed – it's also a handsome building and is used for all sorts of cultural activities. The paintings of Vincent, who once cut off his ear to send to a woman, are as vibrant today as they were when he painted those famous sunflowers and scenes of life in Southern France. The paintings are arranged in chronological order so that you follow his work from early examples to his strange late canvases where blazing stars are suspended in fiery skies and menacing crows flap over flaming wheatfields. You can also see a selection of his letters and drawings.

Amsterdam has always had links with the Far East, notably Indonesia, which it colonized and used for many years. You can see vestiges of Dutch colonialism in the restaurants of Amsterdam – the Indonesian ones are famous, mostly inexpensive and full of character. Try a rice table dinner for a parade of dishes! Or try the Tropenmuseum (Tropical Museum) on Linnaeusstraat for a view of the art of the Far East – not only are there paintings and sculpture but an attempt is made to show what life there is like with music, artefacts, photographs. For maritime Amsterdam the Scheepvaartmuseum (Shipping Museum) on Katenburgerplein has models of ships, maps, paintings, prints and artefacts associated with the sea. It is open every day, but closes at 4 pm.

Amsterdam also boasts a branch of Madame Tussaud's wax museum on Kalverstraat, but this one has a distinct Dutch flavor. It shows historical events and famous citizens of Amsterdam in settings that are all life-size. It's open late on Thursdays.

As well as the already mentioned Amstelkring Museum, there is the Willet

Facing page, top Canvases huge and small cover the walls of the Rijksmuseum, the great treasure house of Dutch art, with great names such as Rembrandt, Rubens, Van Dyke, and Vermeer set beside lesser known masters. Holland's most famous modern painter, Van Gogh, has a museum all his own with a huge array of his works.

Facing page, bottom The Rijksmuseum is situated just beyond the confines of the old city and you can't miss its stately, fanciful façade behind gardens and railings. It's as popular with the Dutch themselves as with tourists. Besides the galleries there is a shop selling reproductions and souvenirs.

Left This is the painter Rembrandt as the sentimental nineteenth century saw him. The old citizen of Amsterdam might have been amused at the graffiti inscribed on the plinth.

Below The Rijksmusuem isn't just paintings, spectacular though the collection is. You will find a host of rooms reflecting the tastes of the seventeenth and eighteenth centuries. Here is a panel of painted glass from Amsterdam's Golden Age.

Holthuysen Museum at 605 Herengracht if you would like to peep inside a seventeenth-century mansion. There's a collection of antique furniture, gold, silver, pottery and fine porcelain. Be sure to look at the period kitchen! The house of the artist Ferdinand Bol can be seen – now it's the Van Loon Museum at 672 Keizersgracht. It offers more a conventional house than a museum, but is only open on Mondays. At the Nieuwe Market you'll find the Jewish Historical Museum housed in the Waag, or Weigh House. Amsterdam even has a museum of piggybanks! There are 12 000 of them in this house on Raadhuisstraat 20, open Monday to Friday. Another museum for specialists is one that houses old gramophones, all working, on the Elandsgracht.

The Westerkerk is where Rembrandt is buried – nobody knows exactly where, although in the north aisle there's a memorial. The Nieuwe Kerk is no longer a functioning church, but is used for concerts. It has a lovely, simple white interior with massive wooden fittings such as the pulpit and the organ case. Still used for state functions, it was the setting for the coronation of Queen Beatrix. It's open every day. The Oude Kerk has been overhauled and restored, but the interior is disappointing – there's a fine view from the tower, though. It's open in summer (not Sundays) and there's an entrance fee. An important (and interesting) Catholic church is St Nicholas near the Zeedijk. This church with an ornate interior is dedicated to the city's patron saint, and there's a procession to celebrate him once a year.

Facing page, above The Dutch fondness of decorative, ornamental frontages can be seen in their public buildings as well as on private houses.

Facing page, bottom The Nieuwe Kerk is a fine high church which is easily found – it is next to the Royal Palace on the Dam Square. It has elegant Gothic windows and, although ornate in style, retains a fittingly simple sense of architectural line.

Left This elaborate organ case can be seen in the Westerkerk. The church tower is a landmark, the tallest in town with a golden crown on the top, presented by an Austrian emperor. Built in 1632, the church has vast brick gables.

The Royal Palace was built not as a royal residence but as a Town Hall, and the ponderous stone building stands on hundreds of piles driven into the mud below. Visit the palace for the interior, however – it gives an impressive sense of Amsterdam's Golden Age in its grandiose salons and staircases, its sculptures and its paintings. It became a royal palace when Napoleon's brother lived here briefly as king in the early nineteenth century. Much of the gilded Empire furniture still to be seen on display was his – he left it when he abdicated in 1810. Do look for the courtroom where once Amsterdam's judges sat and delivered their sentences, while the grand and florid Citizens' Hall proclaims how strong and proud Amsterdam was 300 years ago.

Other places to see Amsterdam as it was are the Amsterdam Historical Museum (on Kalverstraat) with its Civil Guard gallery, a brilliant piece of architecture displaying large canvases of sixteenth- and seventeenth-century Dutch worthies in a wide, glassed-in corridor. The Six Collection at 218 Amstel has fine Rembrandts and paintings by Hals. Other galleries beyond Amsterdam at principal cities such as The Hague (with its marvelous Mauritshuis) and Haarlem (where there are many canvases by Frans Hals) show that the people of Holland may not be wearing the same clothes as they were three centuries ago, but otherwise their faces and figures have hardly changed since the Golden Age.

5
The People

Although the conventional idea of a native Hollander as a straightforward, easy-going, liberal-minded person is basically correct, there is a lot more to the Dutch than that – at least as applied to the Dutch who make Amsterdam their home! The city is an unusual place, probably the most "laid back" in Europe, and it has a great many young people in its population. That's evident when you stroll along any street or sit at a café in any square – it gives the city an air of freedom, lightness and a sense of a place in quest for pleasure. People from all over the world come here in search of fun and the easy-going atmosphere of a great city. The liberal past of Amsterdam shines on in the easy acceptance of pursuits that in other places might be damned, or made furtive. Liberal attitudes are reflected in Dutch history – to take just one event, the February Strike during World War II when Amsterdamers attempted to prevent the Nazis from deporting thousands of Jews from the old Jewish quarter. This was unparalleled in German-occupied Europe, and although it did not succeed it was a brave gesture typical of Holland. Another facet is the acceptance of places of sexual entertainment such as cinemas and bookshops, and the fact that Amsterdam is *the* place in Europe for homosexual bars and clubs, with a large number of people visiting the city to go to these establishments which, for the most part, are clustered around the Muntplein and the Rembrandtsplein. There is even a national center, the COC, for the dissemination of information to gay people, both men and women, at Rozenstraat 14. The native Amsterdamer merely smiles and shrugs his or her shoulders and continues the philosophy of his city – "live and let live".

You will also find the opposite of this attitude in some small Dutch villages where a very tight rein is held on life due to the rigid observance of religion. They are, however, tiny settlements, and bigotry is not something you are likely to come up against in the city. Indeed the over-riding

Street corner encounter – though whether something is being sold, or the occasion is merely a social chat is hard to tell! You can buy all sorts of things on the sidewalks of Amsterdam from salted herrings to a special kind of doughnut.

impression is of politeness and warmth. Some people say that the usual tourist image of a generous warmth and hospitable approach is not the whole story – that there also exists in the Amsterdam character a driving aggressiveness, sometimes expressed in rudeness and minor violence to each other. They put this down to the fact that the city is as tightly crowded as it is possible for a town to be, with people virtually living on top of each other.

I don't think anyone visiting Amsterdam for a short time will carry away this impression. I've always found it a well-mannered and civilized city. Certainly as you walk around the center you'll find no sense of menace, rather the reverse – and of course the fact that wherever you turn English seems to be spoken with a fluency that is embarrassing to a non-Dutch speaker helps make the place even more attractive to the first-time visitor. When shopping there is always assistance, and when you ask for directions on the street it's unlikely that you'll be met with anything else than a kindly courtesy with perhaps a touch of curiosity too, for the Dutch like to know where people come from and what they are doing in Holland.

There is a wide belt of industrial activity around the city which will not interest the visitor much, although certain parts such as the enormous flower market just beyond the suburbs have a good deal of fascination. As you come into Amsterdam from the airport at Schiphol (an airport actually below sea level, and one whose name literally means a place for ships!) you will see much of suburban Amsterdam. In truth it is fairly uniform, gray and not very exciting. Here, however, live the vast mass of the city-dwellers, often traveling on the new underground system into the central city to work. To meet local people you only need to climb onto a suburban train, or a streetcar, or take your bicycle into the hurrying morning or evening throng! You may wonder where the people work when they get into the city, for except for a few hotels there are almost no high-rise

Left Almost like a street in the USA, this busy thoroughfare is filled with shoppers and overhung with a maze of street signs. The Damrak is home for many international businesses and crowded by day and night.

Left On special occasions people still wear national costume, but you will have to look hard to find any in the cities. Here women wearing the famous starched caps look out of a window at a passing parade.

Below The large and ornate street organs are a feature of the city, wheezing out old and new songs. Brilliantly decorated with flowers, figures and painted scenes, they always seem to be fresh and bright.

buildings in the center. Look carefully at the older houses and you will see that many have been adapted for use as offices, old brick façades covering modern facilities.

Fishing is still very much an occupation of the Dutch, and so is the processing of fish – you can see people eating pickled herrings from streetcorner stands. Along the street markets are many stalls selling vegetables and fruits – market gardens (or truck farms) can be found just beyond the suburbs, and if there isn't a garden in a city house then the Amsterdamer will have plants on the balcony, the terrace, the windowbox – even on the ledges of boats on the canal!

Bars and restaurants abound in Amsterdam. Just about everything can be found from delectable open sandwiches to fast-food outlets – note that French fries are usually served smothered in mayonaise! Cheap food is available in student restaurants or "mensas", and most regular restaurants offer a tourist menu at a set price. Dutch food by and large is not exciting, but it *is* wholesome and it comes in large portions. Bars are good value – some serve good snacks, including thick and nourishing soups in winter. Don't miss visiting a "brown bar" – which is something of an Amsterdam institution. Here, in these usually brown-walled establishments, you'll find a convivial atmosphere and you can try Dutch beer or the commonly drunk spirit, Genever gin, taken neat in a small glass. Coffee is good and strong, and you'll even get Dutch cheese for breakfast – a hearty meal of cold cuts, boiled eggs, bread and the very good Dutch butter.

Top The Dutch are great eaters – and besides their own products they import many foodstuffs. Here a cheesemonger cuts into a block, against a background of smoked sausages.

Right Santa Claus is known in Holland as Saint Nicholas, and every year early in December the Saint, complete with flowing white locks, goes on parade in the city from his church. He wears the mitre and carries the crozier of a bishop.

Above Fish is very popular in Holland, and besides fresh supplies from the North Sea there are many smoked and pickled kinds. The Dutch also love smoked eels which are a national delicacy and well worth trying.

Left A rice-table, or rijstafel, is a popular choice for meals in Holland. The dishes are Indonesian, and number anywhere from fifteen up, eaten of course with a mound of rice. The Dutch connection to the Far East goes back over three centuries.

Right The 'girls' don't usually live in their rosily-lit quarters, but come in for work from the suburbs. Often they will display various fetish objects associated with their particular talents beside them in the wide windows.

Below The red light district really does glow crimson when darkness falls!

You should take one of the canal trips—even if it does seem very touristy—for you'll see the city from a different viewpoint, and if it's an evening cruise then the many humped bridges are lit up with electric bulbs. On street corners you'll often find a vast, floridly painted organ, wheezing out popular tunes—a good subject for photos too! You may well come across a street demonstration—Amsterdamers are often devoted to causes and turn out to march or just to enjoy themselves. At night the city is busier than ever—local people come out for a stroll along the shopping street (Kalverstraat is always crowded) or a wander through the red light district. This is the time to have a coffee or a drink on the terraces of one of the squares—a popular one is the Leidseplein in the theater district, near a famous hotel, the "American", which is a monument to art deco and has a handsome café. There will be tourists, true, but many of the walkers and cycle-riders will be local people, out for a bit of air and the pleasure of strolling in a city that doesn't believe wheels are the only way to move!

Right A trip to a diamond cutter is a must when you visit Amsterdam. Diamonds are big business in the city.

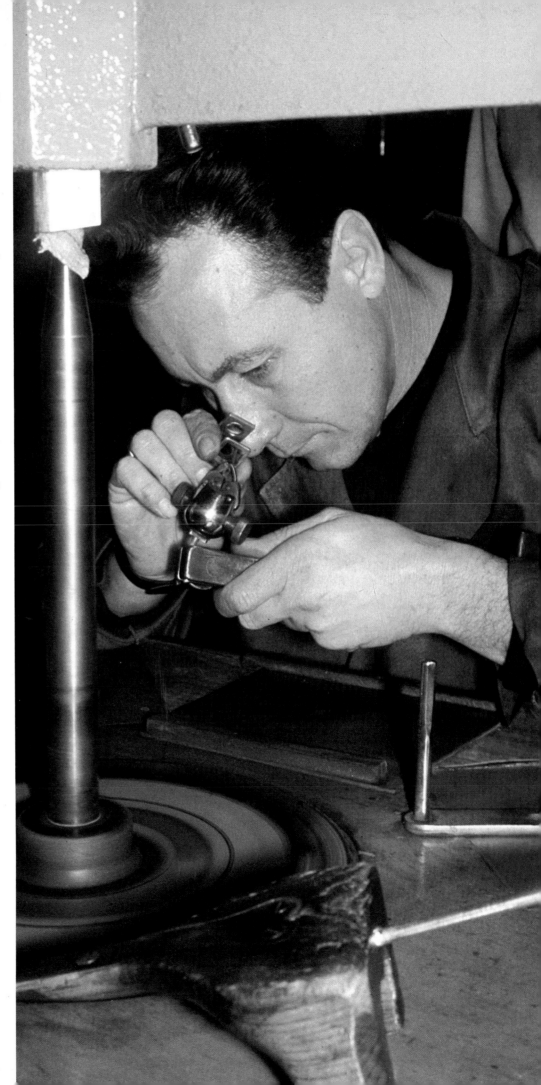

Previous page A corner butcher's shop, small, clean and welcoming and stuffed with good things to eat. The Dutch are often large of figure, and you will understand why when you see how generous helpings of food can be!

Right Even the elderly use bicycles, although sometimes the furious pace of the mass of cyclists along the special tracks necessitates a brief rest!

Below Fishing is popular, and there are lots of places in a watery city like Amsterdam! On Sundays you will see many fishermen out angling in the countryside.

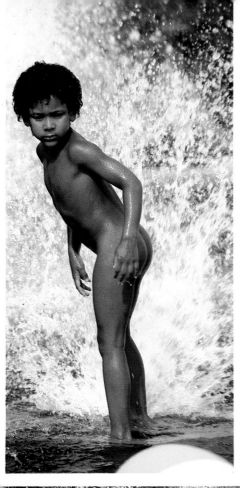

Left Time to cool off! Amsterdam has a large population of people from the old one-time colonies of her Far Eastern lands. Generally the newcomers have assimilated well into their new surroundings.

Below The Vondel Park in the center of the city is a popular gathering place for all sorts of activities and a visit to the charming park with its wide lawns, shady trees and ornamental lakes will show the citizens at leisure.

6

Trips from Amsterdam

Nothing is very far from anything else in Holland. In a small compact country with excellent transport services you can go to numerous places from Amsterdam for a comfortable day, or even half-day, trip. By car, by train, by bus, or even by bicycle (the special tracks extend over a countrywide network and are well-used), Amsterdam's countryside is within easy reach whether you want to see the famous bulbfields ablaze with spring colors, or spend a day in Delft. In this small city, along tree-shaded canals, are all the views you expect of Dutch towns – brick walks, bridges, a busy market – and of course there is the famous Delft blue pottery. If you like this primitive-style blue and white ceramic, then make sure you buy a good sample for there are a lot of cheap reproductions on sale. There's a museum of Delftware, the Lamber van Meerten Museum, if you want to see what it should really look like. The church is a popular one and you can climb the tower for a view – a fee is charged for entry to the kerk where the Dutch royal family have their mausoleum. Delft has a problem, like Volendam just north of Amsterdam: it's too popular. If you go in the spring and summer months expect crowds and an expertly controlled tourist milieu at Volendam, where baggy-panted sailors stroll along the quay, and women wear the black dresses and starched lace caps that one associates with the national costumes of Holland. It's not for the discriminating – try Monnickendam or Edam for more character and less obvious tourist appeal. At Edam there's a cheese market where you can watch the round red cheeses being piled up, and if you select carefully you'll be able to buy the ones the crafty Dutch don't export. If you want to hear the clump of clogs on cobbles and see other Dutch costumes, then try Marken, which was once isolated in the wide gray expanse of the Zuider Zee that the Dutch have been energetically filling in for centuries. Explore

Amsterdam probably looked like this centuries ago, before prosperity dictated the palatial residences of the seventeenth century. The small village of Enkhuisen is reflected in a still harbor pool – more formal house fronts are on the other side of these picturesque tile and brick buildings.

Right Marken is a local village much visited by visitors to Amsterdam – it is on a small green island reached by a causeway. Here it is in winter dress, but the local band still parade in voluminous black pants and clogs.

on your own, using your own transport, if you want to find something of "the real Holland".

To the west of Amsterdam is Haarlem. Filled with interest, this town is about ten miles from Amsterdam and it's worth a whole day for the churches. The huge St Bavo should be seen – its interior is plain but very impressive. At the other end of the Grote Markt, or great market square, is the Town Hall, or Stadhuis. You can visit this handsome edifice, which is actually composed of several styles and dates, and, standing in the great hall, imagine the history it has seen. Frans Hals lived in Haarlem for his last years, dying in penury, and much of his work remained in the city and is now housed in the Frans Hals Museum (open every day). Hals lived at the Oudemannhuis, one of several almshouses erected for the care of the elderly. You can visit most of these charity hospitals, for although still in use their courtyards are usually open.

Another cheese market is at nearby Alkmaar, and Friday is the day to see the energetic porters in their festive dress carting around the wheels of Gouda and piling them on the antique weighing machine at the Waag, or Weigh House. There's a cheese museum here, and at the Stedlijk you can see reconstructions of the sixteenth-century siege when the people of Alkmaar defied the Spanish armies. If you want to buy cheese to take home, remember that Gouda and Edam are not the only Dutch cheeses; there are others closely allied that aren't so mild-tasting and sometimes have added flavorings.

Naarden is an unusual island of a town – a veritable museum of fortifications, most of them constructed 300 years ago. Go up the tower of the Grote Kerk to view these walls and ramparts. Spare some time to look around this church and its ceiling paintings. Nearby is the small riverside settlement of Muiden with its castle, the Muiderslot, while in the opposite direction

is Hilversum with radio and television masts and some unusual modern architecture.

The Hague, where the parliament sits, is a pleasant, easy-going town with a number of extremely good museums, from the Prisoners' Gate with its macabre instruments of torture to the Mauritshuis where Vermeer's "View of Delft" surprises still with its spacious, other-worldly air. In addition to the various royal residences the main tourist attraction is the miniature town of Madurodam on the city's outskirts.

Nearby Leiden is a university town, lively and pleasant and with some very interesting buildings and museums. Here the Pilgrim Fathers gathered before they sailed to the new land from Plymouth – there's an information center on them. The main archeological museum of Holland is here, the Rijksmuseum van Oudheden.

Close to Leiden are the towns of Utrecht with its great looming church tower, and the small and very atmospheric Gouda. The

Left and below Cheese markets always seem to exercise a fascination for tourists – and although cheese is no longer marketed in the old-fashioned ways these spectacles are still preserved mostly for the benefit of visitors. Both Alkmaar and Gouda have cheese markets on specific days, and you can watch the round globes or flattened wheels being piled up and weighed in the market places.

Below You can't imagine Holland without flowers, and even if you don't get to see the famous bulbfields in early spring, you can still go out to the vast market in the suburbs to watch flowers being sold. Here tulips are prepared for the market.

cheeses are sold on Thursdays in the summer season.

Modern Dutch architecture can be seen at Rotterdam, entirely destroyed in World War II due to its pre-eminence as a port. The Boymans-Van Beuningen Museum is a very good reason for visiting the city – a vast and comprehensive painting collection is housed here. Southeast of Rotterdam is Dordrecht, in the area of windmills. You can still see working mills here and there.

For the flower displays you will need to take a tour of the flat lands south of Haarlem – ribbons of vital color in the spring when the famous tulips set the scene. At other times of the year flowers en masse can be seen at the auctions at Aalsmeer, near to Schiphol airport, every weekday from early in the morning. Tulips are something of a Dutch legend – after exploding in value in the seventeenth century they settled down to make an annual cash drop. A well-known legend is the one about the little boy sticking his finger in the dam and saving Holland; you can see his statue at Spaarndam, a mile or so northeast of Haarlem.

If you can only make one trip out of Amsterdam then try Hoorn – here in a quiet, near-deserted backwater of a town once rich and busy there is a peace and an atmosphere you won't find in the tourist-cluttered places. It's changed a lot since it gave its name to Cape Horn! Now you can meander at will through this charming place and perhaps find a feeling of what Holland was, compared with what it is today as reflected in cosmopolitan and energetic Amsterdam.

Above left The fields are vivid swathes of color when the tulips bloom in April and May. The Dutch have always loved tulips and when 'tulipmania' exploded people paid fortunes for a single bulb.

Below left You are never far from the wide spaces of the Dutch countryside in Amsterdam and good roads and excellent bus services will take you to places like Abcoude, where this fisherman is totally alone with the water and sky.

Right Brilliant stripes of color from the air, great ribbons ruled across the flat fields from a car; tulips provide a breathtaking spectacle when they have their short blooming life. Even the old grey barge looks festive!

Holland in miniature – the tiny town of Madurodam where everything is small. The scale of the tourist attraction, near the Hague, can be gauged by the group of visitors on the left of the picture.

Right On the Ijsselmeer a fisherman works in an age-old way, mending his nets by hand. Most fishing now is done on huge factory ships but here at Enkhuizen old trades are still practised.

Below There are still many canals in use as commercial waterways. Amsterdam has a vast shipping canal – the North Sea Canal, handling many ships in a vast dock area. The flatness of the land makes water transport a natural way of getting goods around: over a quarter of Holland's area is said to be navigable waterways.

Facing page Windmills – yes, you *can* see them and within half an hour from the city's center some still functioning, although most of them are now redundant. At one time Amsterdam had many windmills around the city, too.

Major Attractions

1 Royal Palace and Dam Square, National Monument The impressive Royal Palace and the National Monument to Dutch victims of World War Two are in the largest square in the old part of town, on the site of the original Dam.

2 Nieuwe Kerk Begun in 1408, and much damaged by fire on several occasions, the New Church has a simple white interior and attractive wood carvings.

3 Oude Kerk Consecrated in 1306, the Old Church has a 223-foot wooden tower and three beautiful stained-glass windows.

4 Rijksmuseum The most important Dutch museum, it houses collections of furniture, porcelain, glass, sculpture and so on, as well as the most complete selection of Dutch paintings in the Netherlands..

5 Anne Frank House Anne Frank, who kept the famous diary, hid here from the Nazis in World War Two.

6 Rembrandt's House The house was built at the beginning of the seventeenth century, and Rembrandt lived here from 1639 to 1658.

7 Van Gogh Museum This handsome building houses a large collection of paintings and drawings, and is used for a variety of cultural activities.

8 Amsterdam Historical Museum A fascinating collection, representing the city from its earliest beginnings.

9 Central Station Designed by Cuypers in the Dutch Renaissance style, the station is a remarkable landmark, and was built on artificial islands and 900 piles.

10 Begijnhof One of the quaintest squares of Amsterdam, with its charming almshouses and green it preserves the atmosphere of a medieval village.

11 Flower Market This is a colorful and bustling scene much enjoyed by visitors from all parts of the world.

12 Mint Tower The graceful Mint Tower (where coins were made long ago) has the quiet elegance of the Golden Age.

13 Heineken Brewery Where the lager comes from!

14 Westerkerk Rembrandt's burial place, the Western Church has one of the highest and most beautiful towers in Amsterdam.

15 Jewish Museum This symbol of Dutch religious and racial tolerance is in the old weighing house.

16 Vondel Park This pleasant park with its lakes and shady trees is named for Joost van den Vondel, the seventeenth-century poet, Holland's Shakespeare.

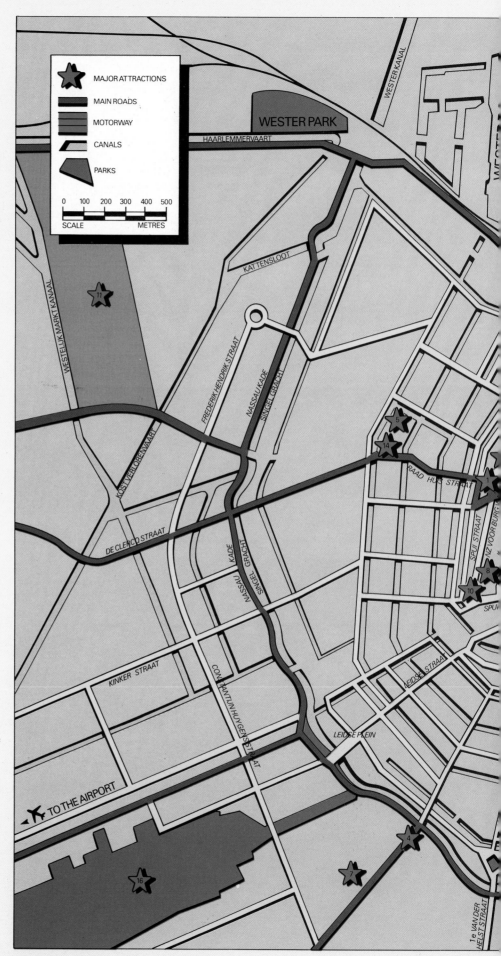

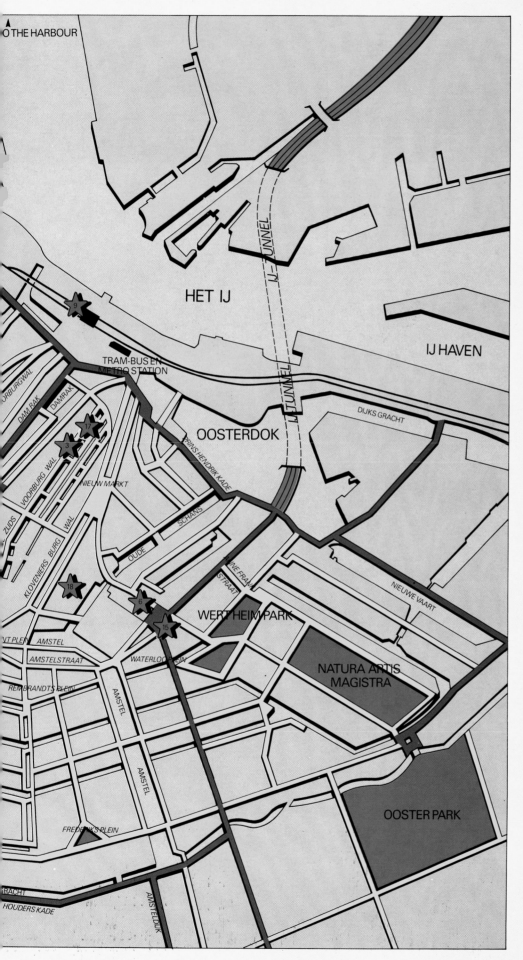

17 Amstelkring Museum "Our Lord in the Attic": the museum of a secret Catholic chapel constructed in a long attic over three houses.

18 Trippenhuis Built by the wealthy Mr Tripp for his coachman, it was only as wide as the merchant's own front door!

O THE HARBOUR

HET IJ

IJ HAVEN

TRAM-BUS EN METRO STATION

OOSTERDOK

DIJKS GRACHT

IJ-TUNNEL

L-TUNNEL

VOORBURGWAL

DAM RAK

DAMRAK

ZIJDS

VOORBURG WAL

NIEUW MARKT

PRINS HENDRIK KADE

KLOVENIERS BURG WAL

SCHANS

OUDE

NIEUWE VAART

STRAAT

WERTHEIM PARK

AMSTEL

NT PLEIN

AMSTELSTRAAT

WATERLOO PLEIN

NATURA ARTIS MAGISTRA

REMBRANDTS PLEIN

AMSTEL

AMSTEL

OOSTER PARK

FREDERIKS PLEIN

HOUDERS KADE

AMSTELDIJK

RACHT

PICTURE CREDITS